Nothing is more precious

than a true friend.

Rachael Hale is an award-winning,
internationally recognised photographer
who specializes in animal portraiture.

Her creative flamboyance with her subjects
has created a new genre in animal photography
and her images have been published
on greetings cards, calendars, posters,
stationery and books worldwide.

Rachael lives in Auckland, New Zealand,
with her three cats Edmund, Gianni and Versace.

NOTHING IS MORE PRECIOUS THAN A TRUE FRIEND
© 2005 Rachael Hale Photography Ltd.
All rights reserved. Rachael Hale is a registered trademark of
Rachael Hale Photography Limited.
www.rachaelhale.com

Edited by J. Rose Barber
Photography courtesy of RACHAEL HALE PHOTOGRAPHY LTD.
Design by WPL

Printed in China
Published by WPL 2005

ISBN 1-904264-28-X

WPL
The Perfume Factory
140 Wales Farm Road
London W3 6UG
Tel: +44 (0) 208 993 7268
Fax: +44 (0) 208 993 8041
email: info@wpl.eu.com
www.wpl.eu.com

One can do without people,
but one has need of a friend.

[CHINESE PROVERB]

Many people will walk in and out of your life,
but only true **friends**
will leave footprints in your **heart**.

[ELEANOR ROOSEVELT]

Friendship can come from

the most unlikely of places.

[WILFRED P. LAMPTON]

...true friends are a sure refuge.

[ARISTOTLE]

Wherever you are it is your friends

who make your world.

[WILLIAM JAMES]

A life filled with

friendship is a good life.

[J. ROSE BARBER]

Friendship is the only cement that will ever hold the world together.

[WOODROW WILSON]

Those who find a friend find treasure.

[IRISH PROVERB]

What is a **friend** ?

A single soul dwelling in two bodies.

Tell me your friends

and I'll tell you who you are.

[ASSYRIAN PROVERB]

The only way to have a friend is to be one.

[RALPH WALDO EMERSON]

A single rose

can be my garden…

a single friend, my world.

[LEO BUSCAGLIA]

Friendship soothes the soul.

[JACQUELINE FRANCIS]

Nothing can come between true friends.

[EURIPIDES]

Happiness is made to be shared.

[AUDREY GRIFFITH]

Friendship is a sheltering tree.

[SAMUEL TAYLOR COLERIDGE]

A true friend thinks of you when all others are thinking of themselves.

[ANON]

Without **friends**,

the world is but a wilderness.

[ANON]

Some people make the world
more special just by being in it.

If you have one true friend
you have more than your share.

[THOMAS FULLER]

Where there is **friendship**,
there is **happiness**.

[FRANCES WICKHAM]

Friendship bears all things, believes all things,

hopes all things, endures all things...

Friendship never ends.

[ADAPTED FROM CORINTHIANS 1]

A **friend** is someone

who understands your past,

believes in your future

and accepts you today

just the way you are.

[PROVERBS 27:17]

A real **friend** is one who walks in

when the rest of the world walks out.

[WALTER WINCHELL]

When they are real, friendships are not glass threads or frost-work, but the solidest thing we know.

[RALPH WALDO EMERSON]

A joy shared is a joy doubled.

[GOETHE]

Friendship is love with understanding.

[AUTHOR UNKNOWN]

Friendship created in a moment
can last a lifetime.

[ROSE ALLEN]

Nothing is worth more than friendship.

[RICARDO PHILIPS]